Outstanding Women of the Bible

Miriam

A woman who saw the answer to her prayers

Retold by Marlee Alex
Illustrated by Florence Magnin

William B. Eerdmans Publishing Company
Grand Rapids, Michigan

MIRIAM
A woman who saw the answer to her prayers
Retold by Marlee Alex
Illustrated by Florence Magnin
© Copyright 1987 by Scandinavia
Publishing House, Nørregade 32, DK-1165 Copenhagen K.
English-language edition published 1988
through special arrangement with Scandinavia
by WM. B. Eerdmans Publishing Co.,
255 Jefferson Ave. S.E., Grand Rapids, Michigan 49503
Printed in Hong Kong
ISBN 0-8028-5030-8

Presenting the Outstanding Women of the Bible

The Bible is the story of God's dealings with his people. This story is like a picture God painted for all the world to see. God wanted to show everyone, everywhere, how much he loves ordinary people, and how he can make wonderful things happen through ordinary lives.

Israel was a nation with laws and traditions which gave men the leadership in government and family life. However, Israel's history is full of stories of women. Some of these women rose to become leaders. Others shaped and changed the life of their nation as they stayed in the background. These stories stress the unique influence women can have on history.

In Israel, the influence of women might have been limited by the customs and laws of their country, or by personal things such as the amount of money they had, the type of education, their husband's position, or the number of children in the family. But in these stories we meet woman after woman who, in spite of outward hindrances, was limited only by the degree of her faith in God or by the degree of her determination to use the gifts he gave her.

We hope this book will make you eager to be used by God, and help you to believe more than ever before that you can be all God made you to be.

Throw every baby boy into the Nile River," Pharaoh ordered. "Let the crocodiles have them or let them drown!"

Pharaoh was a powerful and cruel king. He was cruel because he was terribly afraid. Although he had made the Hebrew people living in Egypt his slaves, over the years they had become too plentiful. They kept having large families and were becoming a strong people. And Pharaoh was afraid someday they might become too powerful to control.

Hebrew mothers shrieked as their baby boys were torn from their arms. The king's soldiers showed no mercy. But one mother whispered to her oldest child, "Miriam, my dear daughter, help me braid these reeds. We are going to make a basket sealed with tar that will float. Your baby brother will just fit inside it. We'll hide the basket among the reeds in the river."

Miriam began to cry. "Mother, how can we set him out on the river? He will drift with the current and be lost. Why, he's just grown big enough to smile at me!" Teardrops splashed down on Miriam's bare feet.

"We must be brave," replied her mother. "This way your brother has a chance to survive. Perhaps the God of our fathers will make a way to spare his life."

Some of Miriam's friends had seen their baby brothers carried away to be killed. Miriam knew her mother was right. "But Mother," she said, drying her eyes, "at least let me watch over the basket from the shore. Then maybe I can see what happens to him. I won't let anyone see me. I promise."

Miriam's mother wrinkled her brow and sighed as Miriam pleaded, "Please mother, please!"

"All right," conceded her mother. "But stay well hidden."

Miriam bent down and lifted her little brother from his mother's breast. He was full and sleepy. She nestled him under the soft blankets in the basket, but her hands were trembling. Looking into the watery eyes of her mother, she said, "Don't be sad. I'm helping. I'll do my best."

Together Miriam and her mother covered the basket and started off toward the river. Along the street they passed a small company of the king's soldiers, marching from house to house. Miriam heard one of the soldiers say, "There was another infant born to a family around here somewhere." Then he stopped Miriam's mother, "Hey woman, tell us! Who has a new baby in this neighborhood? The king's orders are to kill every baby boy."

For a moment Miriam's mother was speechless. But Miriam chirped, "Come, let's get this basketful of dirty clothes washed." She pulled on her mother's skirts.

Then Miriam's mother got an idea. She did not want to lie to the soldiers. But she had to protect the life of her child asleep in the basket. "I hope to hear soon that the baby has been delivered," she replied. And in one way she was right, for she was hoping God would deliver her baby boy from death.

The soldiers grumbled, "We'll be back next week," as they marched off again.

At the river's edge Miriam pulled the basket
cradling her baby brother into the thick
bulrushes. "Lord, protect my baby brother,"
she prayed. "Let him live. Let him grow up."

Miriam's mother pulled leaves and branches around the basket and turned back toward home. Her body shivered, but not from the cold. Miriam stayed hidden, pretending to wade in the shallow water. She pushed her bare toes into the wet sand along the shore. "Let him live. Let him live," she prayed.

The small braided basket was rocked by the gentle river current. Gradually it rocked loose of the reeds and rushes where it had been placed. It began to drift slowly downstream. Miriam followed from the shore, stopping whenever the basket became lodged among the reeds. She wondered, "What shall I do when the basket floats so far away I can no longer follow?"

But Miriam's worries were suddenly interrupted by the giggling and chatter of girls not much older than herself. They were running toward the river. "Ohhh!" gasped Miriam out loud. "The princess!" Miriam could see by the girl's pretty dress that this was the king's daughter. The princess and her handmaidens were coming to bathe at the river. Miriam was afraid she had been discovered by them. Splashing in the water, she hoped the princess would believe she was only playing. "If only they do not notice the basket nearby," she thought.

But the noise had awakened Miriam's baby brother. "Waaa, waaaaa," he cried. The princess immediately saw the little reed basket, half-hidden by river foliage. "Look! Someone has hidden a baby here in the river!" she exclaimed. "This must be one of the Hebrew babies!"

"Isn't he sweet?" cried one of her servants as she dragged the basket to the shore. "The poor little fellow is hungry."

Miriam's heart beat wildly. Her mind was racing. What if the princess took the baby to her father, the cruel king?

Miriam pretended to act as surprised as the other girls at the discovery of the baby. She stepped forward. "If the baby is hungry, I know a mother who can give milk," she told them. "Shall I go and fetch her for you?"

"Why, yes!" exclaimed the princess. "Run along and get her. I will pay her to feed and care for this baby until he is old enough to live with me at the palace. I will raise him as my own son and my father will not hurt him." The princess cuddled the baby in her arms. "His name will be Moses, because I drew him out of the water," she said.

Miriam ran back to her mother as fast as the wind. "He did it!" she shouted. "The Lord has answered our prayers!" That day Miriam's mother was given back her own baby to love and care for until he was old enough to walk, talk, and eat by himself.

any years passed. Miriam grew up. And so did her little brother. But for most of his life Moses had lived like a prince in the beautiful palace, while Miriam and her parents had been slaves of the cruel king.

The king made all the Hebrews' lives miserable. He forced them to work for him all day in the hot sun. They carried heavy loads of grain from the fields and made endless piles of bricks out of straw and mud. Each year the king gave them more back-breaking jobs. He forced them to build great cities and monuments in Egypt.

Miriam spent most of her days in huge vats, tramping water clay and straw with her bare feet. Beads of sweat formed on her face and ran down her neck. Sometimes she paused and looked toward the distant palace where her younger brother lived. Once she even caught a glimpse of him, now a strong young man, walking on the balcony. His jeweled rings and golden arm bands gleamed in the sunlight.

Miriam looked down at her own tattered clothes and thin form. "Dear Lord," she cried out loud, "our people are wasting away in this hot, cruel land. Even our young people grow thinner and weaker day by day. Listen to our groans!"

"Hey, you! Slave!" snarled one of the Egyptian slave drivers. "Keep moving!" His whip cracked through the air and stung Miriam's arm. "Double time!" he barked.

Miriam bit her tongue to keep from yelping. She choked on her own tears. She had seen other slaves whipped to death for complaining. Miriam kept her eyes on the Egyptian palace and began to tramp the clay even harder. "Moses is in there somewhere," she remembered. And that thought brought her comfort. "God, help us, all of us," she prayed silently. Then her eyes searched the palace for yet another glimpse of gold gleaming in the sunlight.

One day Miriam and her family heard some terrible news. Several neighbors were standing outside talking. "The princess's son has killed an Egyptian slave driver!" one said.

"Yes," another answered. "He hid the dead body in the sand, thinking no one would find out!"

"But haven't you heard?" questioned a third neighbor. "Moses has already fled from Egypt. He left the palace in quite a hurry. He must be so scared."

Miriam was paralyzed with shock. "Moses has left Egypt? What will become of him?" she wondered. "And what will become of the rest of us?"

Miriam tried to remember the stories her father had told her as a child. She knew that long ago Abraham, Isaac, and Jacob had been promised a land flowing with milk and honey. God had promised to give this rich land to their children's children, the Hebrew people.

Miriam called upon the Lord again, "Where is this land? When will your promise be fulfilled? How can our people be set free?"

As the hard years slowly rolled by, God seemed deaf to Miriam's cries. But she kept praying. And as she did, her faith in God's promise became strong and sure. The Egyptian palace looked empty and cold without Moses, but the promised land of her dreams grew more dear and more clear. Miriam spoke to her people, the Hebrew slaves, about this promise. She encouraged them to believe, although the fulfillment seemed impossible. She became a prophetess for her people.

One extraordinary day, Moses showed up again at the doorstep of the Egyptian palace. His face was sunburned and wrinkled. His hands were scratched by the thorny bushes of the desert. "Pharaoh," he declared, "the Lord says you must let my people go!"

Pharaoh did not know who this man was. "Who are you and who is the Lord?" he laughed. "You are wasting my time. Go away!"

The news of Moses' return spread quickly among the slaves. When Miriam heard of it she jumped for joy. "Surely this is God's work," she told the others.

But most of the Hebrew slaves were not impressed. "Who does Moses think he is?" they asked. "Does he want to rule over us now himself?"

When the Egyptian slave masters heard of Moses' demand they began to treat the Hebrews even more brutally than before. "You lazy fools," they shouted. "From now on you don't get any more straw to make bricks with. Find straw yourselves if you can! But keep making just as many bricks as before." The whips of the slave masters ripped the shirts off the backs of any who grumbled.

Miriam went out into the hay fields to search for stubble which she could mix with her vat of clay. Late that night she was still working, trying to finish making her daily quota of bricks. The next day when the bricks had dried, they crumbled and broke, for there had not been enough straw to make the clay strong. Miriam's dreams for a better life seemed to be crumbling just like her bricks.

Moses stayed in Egypt, however, insisting that Pharaoh let the Hebrews go. God struck Egypt with one terrible plague after another. Yet Pharaoh continued to refuse the Hebrews their freedom because he wanted all the slaves he could get.

Then Moses told his own people, "Tonight the shadow of death will pass over Egypt and strike down the firstborn of every Egyptian family. But you are to slaughter a lamb at twilight and with its blood paint the doors of your homes. When the Lord sees the blood, He will pass over you, and death shall not touch those who sleep within."

Miriam and her family carefully poured the blood of a lamb into a basin. They dipped a branch of hyssop into it and smeared the blood onto the doorjamb of their hut. Then they put on their cloaks, tied up their sandals, and waited for the shadow of death to pass by their home.

At midnight the air seemed suddenly cold and damp. Miriam shuddered as the sound of loud weeping and wailing came from the windows of Egyptian neighbors. By the very early hours of the morning there was not one Egyptian family who had not lost a child. Even Pharaoh's oldest son died that night. But the Hebrew children slept unharmed, and among them not a dog barked.

While it was still dark Pharaoh stumbled out onto his balcony and shouted, "Get out, you Hebrews! All of you! Take your little ones and your old ones, your sons and your daughters, your flocks and your herds. Don't let me see a single one of you ever again!" Pharaoh turned back inside the palace, bitterly weeping over the loss of his boy.

As the first rays of dawn pierced the blackness of night, a white pillar of cloud rose from the ground and into the sky. Miriam rubbed her eyes and stared. "Do you see it?" she called to her neighbors. "Do you recognize God in the cloud? He never forgot us. He has come to deliver us from slavery after all!"

Miriam left her home and was hurrying down the street when an Egyptian woman appeared in a doorway. She was the wife of a slave master. The woman threw a heap of golden jewelry at Miriam's feet. "Take this and get out!" she sobbed. "My son is dead. What good is this gold to me now?"

Miriam scooped up the jewelry from the dusty street and hurried on, thinking, "Why, this gold does not sparkle as I thought it did. But we're finally on our way!"

The pillar of cloud now began to move before the huge crowd of Hebrew men, women, children, and animals. God led them through the narrow streets of towns and villages. Then, instead of heading up over the hills, the pillar of cloud moved out into what seemed an endless stretch of hot desert sand.

The gritty sand filled their sandals and lodged between their toes. It was whipped by breezes through their clothes. It stuck in the corners of their eyes. Nor could they keep it out of their food and water. The children cried and complained. "When will we reach the beautiful land?" they asked over and over again. "When will we be across this desert?"

Miriam patted the children's small heads. "Keep your courage up," she said as they tramped onward. She started to hum a familiar tune for them.

But the grownups interrupted, "We are going the wrong way. There is nothing ahead but the sea, and we have no boats with which to cross it."

Then a little girl shouted, "Listen! Don't you hear something?"

"Look! Behind us!" shouted her father. "It's Pharaoh and his horse-drawn chariots!"

The Hebrew crowd panicked. Pharaoh was riding toward them at a furious rate. He had decided not to let them go after all.

FM

The Hebrews cried out to Moses, who was walking out in front of them. "Why did you bring us out here to be pinned down by Pharaoh, trapped between the desert and the sea? We should never have left Egypt!"

Miriam looked into the angry, frightened faces of those she had labored alongside as makers of Egyptian bricks and builders of Egyptian towers. Her eyes met those of a terrified young woman with a baby tied to her back and two other children clinging to her legs. Miriam was wondering, "Can they be right? Are we to die out here?" But Miriam could not forget how God had answered her childhood prayers for Moses and had returned Moses to them two times, once as a baby and once as a leader. "No," she told the young woman, "God has brought us out of Egypt, and He will bring us into a land where there is a bright future for your children."

Moses' voice quieted the entire crowd. "The Lord will fight for you today!" he declared.

As Moses spoke, the pillar of cloud moved behind the people, casting a dark shadow over the approaching Egyptian horsemen. Moses stretched his arm out toward the sea lying before them.

"Come," cried Miriam. "Run! March! Let's go!" The people hurried ahead and stepped into the waves lapping at the seashore. The waves split apart and banked, leaving a dry path across the floor of the sea. All that night the Hebrews fled between the walls of water, across the sea, and onto dry land.

Finally, the last family reached safety. But Pharaoh's chariots were still chasing them. This time Moses stretched his arm out over the sea from the other shoreline, and as he did so the walls of water caved in. The Egyptian soldiers, horses, and chariots were swept away and drowned.

The Hebrews watched what happened as if in a dream. But Miriam dug into her traveling gear and pulled out a tambourine.

She raised it into the air with a shimmy. She dashed it against the palm of her other hand. She began to sway, light as a bubble. In and out among the people she danced as the jingling of the tambourine rang over the sea. Then she began to sing, "Sing to the Lord, for He is great! Sing to the Lord, for He is great!"

The young woman with the baby on her back raised her hands in the air and began to clap to the rhythm. The two children pranced around her feet. Another woman grabbed a tambourine and followed Miriam through the crowd. One by one little girls, weary mothers, and stoop-shouldered old women joined the circle of jubilant dancers, as the men stood nearby and clapped. They all sang the song of Miriam. "Sing to the Lord, for He is great. He has hurled horses and riders into the sea!" The early-morning, desert air was filled with music.

29

The Hebrews were on their way to the Promised Land.

s a child Miriam learned to trust God and to pray. She saw how God answered her prayers for her baby brother, Moses. When she grew up she became a prophetess. She told people about God's ways and encouraged them to believe in Him even when it seemed impossible.

But Miriam was not perfect. Once, during the long journey to the Promised Land, she criticized her brother Moses because she was jealous of him. "Does the Lord speak only through Moses?" she asked. "Doesn't He also speak through me?" The Lord became angry with Miriam, but forgave her when Moses offered up prayers for her.

Miriam will be remembered as an energetic, hardworking woman who trusted the Lord when times were hard and kept faith through many difficult years. Miriam was a woman who saw the answers to her prayers.